Raw Food Recipes

89 Delicious, Easy Beginner Raw Food Recipes for Sustained Energy and Optimal Health

Table of Contents

Introduction

"Don't dig your grave with your own knife and fork." - English Proverb

"Today, more than 95% of all chronic disease is caused by food choice, toxic food ingredients, nutritional deficiencies and lack of physical exercise." - Mike Adams

"The doctor of the future will no longer treat the human frame with drugs, but rather will cure and prevent disease with nutrition." - Thomas Edison

Food is many things to us. It is our sustenance, our comfort, our joy. Without it we would not survive; yet, some of the foods we put into our bodies do not help us be healthy. Foods that have been genetically modified or sprayed with pesticides and herbicides do more harm to the body than good. In this day where so many of our foods have been tampered with, deciding to go raw using organic fruits, vegetables, nuts and seeds can help the body go from being tired and sick to regaining some natural health through food. Raw foods retain many enzymes, vitamins and nutrients that are destroyed when food is cooked over 115°. Even changing the diet to 50% raw foods will help the body repair itself. Many find they have more energy, their skin improves, and they feel better overall.

Raw cooking needn't be too time-consuming or overwhelming. If you are just starting to incorporate more raw food into your diet then try for 1 meal a week. Find out what ingredients you need and prepare for it. Once you get used to creating a meal using only raw food, move to 2 meals a week, and eventually to 1 meal a day. Pretty soon, you'll be making mostly raw meals.

You'll need a few specific appliances and items for raw cooking. These will help you create recipes quickly and easily. Try to eventually invest in some high quality products.

What you will need for cooking:

Dehydrator

Foods can be "cooked" in the dehydrator and still be considered "raw" due to the food temperature never exceeding 115°. Even food cooked at 130° – 145° in a dehydrator won't exceed the 115° limit for raw food, so you still have a raw dish, packed with nutrients. Dehydrators are great for cookies, crackers, crusts, dried fruit, dried herbs, and even veggie burgers!

Blender

A top quality blender is a must for raw cooking. It will create a wonderfully smooth and creamy end product for smoothies, desserts, dressings, soups, etc. I personally use a VitaMix. It is a little on the expensive side and there are definitely other blenders out there; however the VitaMix motor is top quality and they offer a fantastic guarantee, which is why I strongly recommend you eventually invest in a VitaMix. If you already have a good blender to start with, that will be fine. But many motors in the less expensive brands eventually wear out.

Food Processor

You may be asking, "If I have a good blender, do I really *need* a food processor too?"

The short answer is "Yes!"

Blenders are wonderful for creating amazingly smooth recipes; however, you need a food processor to create chunkier recipes such as cookie dough, crusts, crackers, etc.

Your food processor doesn't need to be as expensive as your blender. One in the $50 to $75 range will work great. The only exception is when you make nut butters. They have a tendency to run a motor down due to the long processing times – especially for almond butter. But a good food processor in the above price range should work just fine.

Spiral Slicer and/or Mandoline Slicer

Spiral slicers are perfect for creating vegetable "noodles" from zucchinis, cucumbers, and many other vegetables. These "noodles" are a main ingredient in

wonderful raw dishes such as Italian
Spaghetti and Pad Thai!

Mandoline slicers create thin "chips" that you
can then dehydrate to make crunchy, dried
foods such as dried apples, yams or sweet
potatoes, etc. Mandoline slicers can also
julienne or shred your vegetables and fruits
for many meals.

Nut Milk Bag

A nut milk bag will make creating delicious
nut milks a breeze. It is faster and easier
than a traditional strainer and does a better
job. You can find nut milk bags online.

Not Technically Raw

Some foods claiming to be raw many times are not. There are some ingredients I use that are not fully raw; however, I choose to use them because they add great flavor to my recipes. If you choose to go completely raw with no exceptions, you can easily omit these ingredients and still have wonderful dishes. Here are the few ingredients I use that are "not technically raw":

Vanilla, Almond and Other Extracts

Extracts are typically not considered raw. However, they give great depth and flavor to many recipes, so I choose to use them. There are recipes for raw vanilla extract online. If you'd like to make some to use in your cooking, I suggest the following video.

Raw Vanilla Extract:

http://www.everydaydish.tv/recipe/raw-vanilla-extract

Pure Maple Syrup and Agave Nectar

Pure maple syrup is not raw due to the process of extracting the maple sap and cooking it down over a long period of time. However, I like to use it because it retains many vitamins including Manganese, B vitamins, Calcium and Magnesium, among others. It also contains over 50 antioxidants, and polyphenols, which are anti-inflammatory – not bad for a substance that is boiled extensively!

There has been a lot of controversy over agave nectar. Some say it is not raw and even worse than high fructose corn syrup! While there are products out there that are probably not good for you, I choose to use certain brands of agave because, a) it only takes a small amount to sweeten up a dessert or smoothie, and b) I personally don't believe agave is all bad! There are raw versions of agave and it is important for you to do your own research when it comes to this sweetener; however, there is some information on the following website that squelches a lot of the misinformation out there. You can find it here:

Salt and Other Spices

Traditional store-bought salt is not raw. It is
heated and processed with chemicals – yuck!
However, certain brands of sea salt are
considered raw and are good for you too;
some of which include Himalayan Sea Salt,
Celtic Sea Salt, and Redmond Real Salt.
These salts retain numerous trace minerals
and only take a small amount to flavor a
dish.

Spices may or may not be raw, depending on
how the spice was harvested. Any home
grown herbs or spices can be dried in a
dehydrator and would therefore be
considered raw. As far as market brands are
concerned, just be sure to read each label to
determine the processing.

Nama Shoyu

Nama Shoyu is a Japanese product that is
basically unpasteurized soy sauce. The name
nama means raw (or unpasteurized), and
shoyu means soy sauce. The product is
heated over the 115° that is allowed on a raw

diet; however, many raw foodists allow it because it contains living enzymes.

Oats

There has been some controversy over whether oats are raw or not. Some manufacturers put hulled oats through a heat and moisture treatment, which damages the germ so it won't sprout naturally. Look for naked oats, which means they haven't been through the treatment process. You can find naked oats at most health food stores and online.

Dried Fruit

Unless you dehydrate your fruit yourself at the desired temperature for raw foods of 115° or less, it is not considered truly raw.

Nuts

Even many nuts are lightly pasteurized which means they are not truly raw. You can find true raw nuts online. A great site is:

www.nuts.com/Raw-Nuts

Tahini

Tahini is a paste made from sesame seeds that is very popular in the Middle East. Most commercial versions use toasted sesame seeds; therefore, it is not considered raw. However, it's easy to make a raw version. Just soak 1 cup of seeds in 2 cups water for 5 hours. Drain the water and place in refrigerator for another 5 hours. Then, place the seeds in a high speed blender and puree until a smooth paste forms. Tahini is delicious in many recipes.

A Note About Oils:

Make sure the oils you use are cold-pressed and extra virgin to be truly raw.

As with anything, you must make the judgment call on any food you use.

Special Ingredients

You really don't *need* any special ingredients to eat raw, (there are so many fruits, vegetables, nuts and seeds that you could create a countless number of dishes with different combinations); however, there are a few particular ingredients that can help make your dish go from good to fantastic!

If you can, try to keep these particular ingredients on hand. As you continue to create new and more complex raw recipes, these ingredients may show up more often on the ingredient list:

Nutritional Yeast or Yeast Flakes

Nutritional yeast is a nutty, cheesy flavored inactive yeast that is popular with raw foodists. It gives dishes a deeper and more intricate flavor, and is a good source of vitamin B12.

11

Young Thai Coconuts

Young Thai coconuts are used in many dishes that call for the young meat. The meat in these can range from very soft to hard, depending on the maturity of the coconut. When buying, look for coconuts that have little or no spots or blemishes. Coconuts have numerous health benefits as they are full of vitamins, minerals, antioxidants, enzymes and amino acids, among others.

Hemp Seeds

Hemp seeds are highly nutritious. They are full of amino acids, essential fatty acids and protein. They are delicious in smoothies, desserts, dips, salads, etc.

Chia Seeds

Chia seeds are full of fiber, amino acids, and are a complete protein, providing numerous health benefits, and are perfect in many recipes, often being substituted for flax seeds. Soaking the seeds create a "gel" that can be used in many recipes as a thickener or in place of fats.

Cacao Butter

Cacao butter is the fat that's extracted from the cacao bean. It has a wonderfully rich, delicious taste and is used in many dessert recipes. Cacao butter also has ant-inflammatory effects and is healthy for the heart.

Nama Shoyu

Covered in previous section.

Tahini

Covered in previous section.

There are numerous other ingredients that can be used in a raw diet; these are just a few of some common ones.

Raw Nut Butters, Milks and Sauces

Raw nut butters are delicious and surprisingly easy to make using your food processor and a little patience! They are the perfect high protein snack, and can be spread on dehydrated crackers, vegetable and fruit slices, and used in dehydrated cookies.

Nut milks are highly nutritious, wonderful for breakfasts or just to drink by themselves, and are the perfect alternative to dairy and soy milk. Be sure to experiment with different flavors and spices to create extra delicious milk!

Raw fruit sauces are easy to make and full of nutrients. Use them in recipes or enjoy fresh with a sprinkle of ground cinnamon!

Raw Almond Butter

3 cups raw almonds

Add-ins:

Sea salt

Vanilla Extract

Extra virgin coconut oil

Raw honey

Cacao Powder

Place almonds in a food processor. Turn on Low and blend, stopping to scrape sides occasionally, for anywhere from 10 – 30 minutes. The amount of time needed will depend on the quality of your food processor. The almonds will at first look grainy, then they will begin to bind together (if the almonds form a large ball, simply separate by cutting into fourths and keep processing), and lastly, the processing will extract the oils to create almond butter. You'll know it's done when the butter has an oily look to it. The process is somewhat time-consuming, but the end result is fantastic!

Once almond butter is finished, stir in by hand any extra you'd like. The sea salt gives it a robust flavor, honey adds a sweet aftertaste, while the cacao powder creates a smooth, chocolate nut butter. Experiment and enjoy!

Makes about 1 pint

NOTE: Almond butter is easiest to spread at room temperature; however, to extend freshness, keep in refrigerator and take out a half hour before serving to bring to room temperature.

Raw Peanut Butter

3 cups raw peanuts

2 – 3 Tbsp. extra virgin coconut oil

(peanut and sunflower oil work well too)

Add-ins:

Any add-ins from the Almond Butter recipe

Place peanuts in a food processer. Turn on Low and process until mixture comes together. Add oil a little at a time and continue blending and occasionally scraping the sides until peanut butter is at desired consistency. Any add-ins are wonderful in this butter. You can also substitute 1/2 cup peanuts for another nut to make a mixed nut butter. Almonds, hazelnuts and cashews work well.

Makes about 1 pint

Raw Hazelnut Butter

3 cups raw hazelnuts

Add-ins:

Cacao powder

Raw honey

Vanilla extract

Place hazelnuts in a food processor. Turn on Low and process, scraping sides occasionally, until oils are extracted and hazelnut butter is smooth and creamy. This nut butter is amazing all by itself, but when you stir in cacao (3 Tbsp.), raw honey (3 Tbsp.) and vanilla (1/2 tsp.), it becomes a sinfully delicious chocolate nut butter similar to Nutella.

Makes about 1 pint

Raw Coconut Milk & Flour

1 to 5 mature coconuts (the number you use will determine the thickness of your milk)

3 cups water

Using a meat cleaver, hit the middle of a coconut to crack it. Continue hitting around the middle until the crack is all the way around. The coconut will split in half. Place halves on a cutting board, coconut side down. Again using the cleaver, hit the tops until they crack across the entire half. Remove the hard outer shell and peel or scrape off the brown skin from the coconut flesh. Chop into chunks. Using the flesh from 1 coconut, place it with the water in a high-powered blender (I use a VitaMix). Blend for 4 – 5 minutes. Pour mixture into a nut milk bag and strain well. Save the pulp for coconut flour!

To make thicker coconut milk or coconut cream:

Using the coconut milk from the first blend, add it to the blender with the flesh from a second coconut. Blend 4 – 5 minutes and again, strain. Continue this process depending on how creamy you want your coconut milk.

To make coconut flour:

Dehydrate the pulp at 115° for 3 – 4 hours or until completely dry. Pour into a blender and blend into flour.

Raw Almond Milk

2 cup raw almonds, soaked overnight

6 cups water

4 dates

1 tsp. vanilla or almond extract (if desired)

Sea salt (if desired)

Spices (cinnamon, nutmeg, ginger, etc.)

Place almonds, water and dates in a food processor; blend until creamy. Strain mixture using a nut milk bag. Stir in vanilla and a pinch of sea salt, if desired. You can also add any ground spice to liven up the flavor! Store in refrigerator for up to 1 week. Save the pulp! It is almond meal that can be added to many recipes, including raw cookies and smoothies. Or, you can dehydrate it to make almond flour.

Makes about 6 - 7 cups almond milk

Raw Cashew Milk

2 cups raw cashews

6 cups water

Add-ins:

Vanilla extract

Sea salt

Spices

Place cashews and water in a high speed blender or food processor. Blend until mixture is creamy. Add in any extra if desired. Refrigerate and enjoy!

There is no need to strain cashew milk as cashews are very soft and blend almost completely into the liquid.

Makes about 6 cups cashew milk

Raw Applesauce

6 apples

1 $^1/_2$ cups water

2 tsp. fresh lemon juice

8 Medjool dates, soaked for at least 2 hours

Ground cinnamon

Peel and core apples. Place apples, water, lemon juice and dates in a large food processor or you can divide into 2 batches using a high speed blender. Blend until smooth. Stir in cinnamon to taste.

Optional add-ins: agave, raisins, sliced almonds, nutmeg, coconut.

Makes about 3 cups applesauce

Raw Pear Sauce

6 pears

1 cup water

1 tsp. fresh lemon juice

Core pears and place in a high speed blender. Add water and lemon juice and puree until smooth, adding more water if needed.

Optional add-ins: agave, cinnamon, nutmeg, cardamom, dried fruit, chopped nuts. You can also add a few apples to this to make pear-apple sauce.

Makes about 3 cups pear sauce

Raw Breakfasts

Raw breakfasts are easy to make, taste delicious and give you a perfect start to your day. These flavorful recipes will give you the necessary nutrients your body needs to get your day going. You'll never want to skip breakfast again!

Raw Coconut Banana Maple Oatmeal

2 ½ cups raw oat groats

3 cups water

1/4 cup shredded dehydrated coconut

2 ripe bananas

Pure maple syrup

Ground cinnamon

Combine oats and water and let soak overnight. Pour oat mixture in a high speed blender with the shredded coconut. Puree until smooth. Add bananas and pulse until just combined. Stir in maple syrup and cinnamon to taste.

Serves 6

26

Fruity Tropical Breakfast Salad

1 cup pineapple chunks

1 cup mango chunks

1 cup sliced bananas

1 cup sliced strawberries

1/2 cup shredded dehydrated coconut

1/4 cup dehydrated apricot pieces

1/4 cup chia seeds

1/4 cup flax seeds

3 Tbsp. raw honey

In a large bowl, combine all ingredients and mix well. This salad is wonderful on its own or on top of raw oatmeal.

Serves 4 - 6

Chia "Cold Cereal"

1 cup organic chia seeds

6 cups water

Add-ins:

Raw organic coconut cream

Raw honey

Dried fruit

Chopped nuts

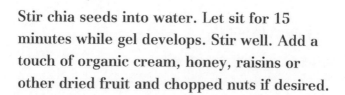

Stir chia seeds into water. Let sit for 15 minutes while gel develops. Stir well. Add a touch of organic cream, honey, raisins or other dried fruit and chopped nuts if desired.

Serves 8

28

Peach Coconut Cream Breakfast Crepes

Crepes:

4 medium bananas

1 – 2 Tbsp. fresh lemon juice

Dash of cinnamon and nutmeg

Filling:

Meat from 2 young Thai coconuts

1/2 cup dehydrated shredded coconut

1 Tbsp. raw honey

1 tsp. fresh lemon juice

1/2 tsp. vanilla extract

2 large peaches, pitted and thinly sliced

For the crepes: Place bananas in a high

speed blender. Turn on Low and slowly pour the lemon juice in through the top until the mixture is smooth and thin. Add cinnamon and nutmeg. Pour out 8 small rounds onto a dehydrator tray lined with parchment paper. Place in dehydrator at 115°. Dehydrate for 6 – 7 hours or until crepes are easy to pick up, yet will fold easily.

For the filling: Place the meat from the young coconuts, shredded coconut, honey, lemon juice and vanilla extract in a food processor. Blend until smooth and creamy. Place a spoonful of filling on each crepe. Top with sliced peaches. Fold crepe over filling and serve.

Serves 6 – 8

Breakfast Dip with Fruit Slices

8 Medjool dates, pitted

1 cup macadamia nuts

1/2 cup raw oats

1 Tbsp. flax seed

1/2 tsp. vanilla extract

1/4 tsp. sea salt

2 – 3 Tbsp. raw almond milk

Fruit slices and chunks such as apple, pear, banana, pineapple, peach, etc.

Soak the dates and macadamia nuts together for about an hour. Place dates, macadamia nuts, oats, flax seed and sea salt in a high speed blender. Puree and slowly add the almond milk to create desired consistency. Serve with sliced fruit for dipping.

Serves 4 – 6

Veggie Breakfast Scramble

1 cup almonds

1 cup hazelnuts

1 cup sunflower seeds

1 cup almond milk

2 tsp. chili powder

1/2 tsp. cumin

Sea salt

1 red bell paper, diced

1/4 cup sliced scallions

2 small tomatoes, diced

Italian parsley

Place the almonds, hazelnuts and sunflower seeds in a food processor; blend until flour forms. Add almond milk, chili powder, cumin and sea salt. Stir in vegetables and sprinkle with parsley.

Serves 4 – 6

Raw Granola with Berries

2 cups buckwheat groats

4 Tbsp. ground flaxseed

1/2 cup chopped almonds

1/2 cup sunflower seeds

1/2 cup dehydrated shredded coconut

1/2 cup pure maple syrup

1/4 cup water

2 Tbsp. extra virgin coconut oil

1 tsp. ground cinnamon

1/2 tsp. vanilla extract

1/2 tsp. maple extract

1/4 tsp. sea salt

1 cup fresh blueberries

1 cup fresh raspberries

Soak the buckwheat groats in water for half an hour; drain and rinse. Place groats, flaxseed, almonds, sunflower seeds and shredded coconut in a food processor; pulse until ingredients are combined. Add the maple syrup, water, coconut oil, cinnamon, vanilla extract, maple extract and sea salt. Again, pulse until combined. Stir in blueberries and raspberries by hand. Spread onto lined dehydrator sheets. Dehydrate at 115° for 20 – 22 hours or until mixture is completely dry and crispy. Serve with almond or coconut milk.

Serves 8

Granola "Yogurt" Parfaits

2 cups fresh blueberries

2 cups Raw Granola with Berries

1 cup raw cashews, soaked for 2 hours

1 ¾ cups raw coconut milk

1/4 cup pure maple syrup

1 tsp. fresh lemon juice

1 tsp. vanilla extract

Pinch sea salt

Dehydrated shredded coconut

Divide blueberries into 6 individual glasses. Evenly divide the Raw Granola over berries. Place the cashews, coconut milk, maple syrup, lemon juice and sea salt in a high speed blender; puree until smooth and creamy. Place a spoonful of "yogurt" cream on each parfait. Sprinkle each with shredded coconut. Refrigerate until ready to serve.

Serves 6

Coconut Avocado Mousse

2 medium avocados, pitted

1 pear, peeled and quartered

1 apple, peeled and quartered

1/2 cup coconut milk

1 – 2 tsp. Agave nectar (to taste)

Shredded dehydrated coconut

Place the avocados, pear, apple and coconut milk in a food processor and blend until smooth. Add agave to taste and top each serving with shredded coconut.

Serves 4

Caramel Cashew Waffles

Waffle Batter:

1 ½ cups flax meal

1 ½ cups cashews, soaked for 2 hours

3 cups buckwheat groats, soaked for 2 hours

Caramel Topping:

1/2 cup cashews, soaked for 2 hours

2 Tbsp. coconut butter

4 - 5 Tbsp. coconut water

3 - 4 Tbsp. pure maple syrup

1 tsp. vanilla extract

Pinch of sea salt

For the waffles: Combine ingredients into a high speed blender and puree until batter looks mildly sticky. Take a waffle iron and cover the bottom with plastic wrap. Spoon some dough onto the wrap and spread evenly. Cover the top with another layer of plastic wrap. Close the waffle iron to make a "waffle". Take out and set on a dehydrator sheet. Repeat this process until you've created 6 large waffles. Place waffles in dehydrator and dehydrate at 110° for about 8 hours.

For the caramel: Combine all ingredients in a high speed blender. Add the coconut water to desired consistency and the maple syrup to taste. Pour sauce on top of waffles.

Serves 6

Pineapple Banana Muesli

1/3 cup raw pecans

1/4 cup raw almonds

1/4 cup pumpkin seeds

1/4 cup dehydrated shredded coconut

12 dates, soaked for 20 minutes

2 Tbsp. extra virgin coconut oil

1 ¹/₂ cups small pineapple chunks

2 medium bananas, sliced in rounds

Almond milk

Combine pecans, almonds, pumpkin seeds, coconut and dates in a food processor; pulse until nuts are broken up and mixture is well combined. Drizzle in coconut oil and pulse a few more times. Top each serving with fruit and almond milk.

Serves 4

Cherry Vanilla Breakfast Pudding

12 Medjool dates, soaked for 2 hours

2 large avocados

1/2 cup almond or cashew milk

1 ½ tsp. vanilla extract

1 cup cherries, pitted and chopped

Chopped pecans (optional)

Combine all ingredients except for pecans in a high speed blender; puree until a smooth, creamy pudding forms. Garnish with chopped pecans, if desired.

Serves 8

Raw Smoothies

Raw smoothies are the perfect way to get any combination of fruits or vegetables in a delicious, healthful drink. Smoothies have been praised by not only raw foodists, but many other health conscious groups due to their amazing benefits, such as: weight loss, increased energy, detoxification, better overall health, improved skin, etc. Another great thing about smoothies is they are very easy and take little time to prepare. Be sure to experiment with different combinations!

Morning Orange Smoothie

2 medium oranges, peeled

1 large peach, pitted

1 banana, peeled

2 stalks celery

1/2 cup raw almond milk

1/2 cup ice

Chop fruits and vegetable into chunks.
Combine all ingredients in a high speed
blender and puree until smooth.

Serves 3 – 4

Ginger Carrot Green Smoothie

4 medium carrots, chopped

1 apple, cored and quartered

1 stalk celery

2 cups chopped spinach, chard or kale

1 – 2 Tbsp. freshly grated ginger root (to taste)

Filtered water and ice

Combine all ingredients in a high speed blender; puree until smooth.

Serves 4

Hemp Berry Smoothie

2 cups frozen berries (medley of blueberries, raspberries, blackberries and strawberries)

2 Tbsp. hemp seed

1 Tbsp. maca

1 medium avocado

1/2 medium cucumber

Filtered water and ice

Combine all ingredients in a high speed blender; puree until smooth.

Serves 4

Fresh Lemony-Green Smoothie

1 cup baby spinach greens

2 stalks celery

1 apple, washed and quartered

1/4 cup chopped fresh parsley

1/2 fresh lemon, rind left on

Filtered water and ice

Combine all ingredients in a high speed blender; puree until smooth.

Serves 2 – 3

Minty Chocolate Smoothie

1 cup coconut milk

2 ripe bananas, peeled

2 cups baby spinach leaves

1 apple, washed and quartered

1 Tbsp. cacao powder

Food grade peppermint essential oil

Filtered water and ice

Combine all ingredients in a high speed blender and puree until smooth. Add the peppermint oil to taste.

Serves 3 – 4

Coconut Pineapple-Lime Smoothie

1 $1/2$ cups pineapple chunks

1 banana

1 medium avocado, pitted

1 lime, peeled

Agave or raw honey (to taste)

1/2 cup coconut milk

Ice

Combine all ingredients in a high speed blender; puree until smooth.

Serves 4

Raspberry Orange Chocolate Smoothie

2 cups loose greens such as kale, chard or beet greens

1 cup fresh raspberries

2 medium oranges, peeled (use the zest from them in the smoothie)

4 bananas, frozen

3 – 4 Tbsp. cacao powder (to taste)

4 Tbsp. hemp seed

1 tsp. agave nectar

Pinch of sea salt

1 ½ cups almond milk

Ice

Combine all ingredients in a high speed blender; puree until smooth.

Serves 4

Greens & Grape Smoothie

3 cups red grapes, washed

3 cups baby spinach leaves

1 banana, peeled

1 apple, cored and quartered

1 Tbsp. chia seed

Water and ice to desired consistency

Combine all ingredients in a high speed blender; puree until smooth.

Serves 4

Cantaloupe Mango Smoothie

1 medium cantaloupe, rind removed

2 mangos, pitted

2 cups baby spinach leaves

1 Tbsp. ground flaxseed

1/2 coconut milk

Ice

Combine all ingredients in a high speed blender; puree until smooth.

Serves 4

Spiced Pumpkin Pie Smoothie

1 cup pureed pumpkin

2 bananas, frozen

2 carrots, sliced

1 ½ cups coconut milk

2 tsp. agave nectar

1 tsp. vanilla extract

1 tsp. ground cinnamon

1/2 tsp. ground nutmeg

1/4 tsp. ground cloves

Ice

Combine all ingredients in high speed blender; puree until smooth. Garnish with an extra sprinkle of cinnamon on each serving.

Serves 4

Passion Fruit Green Smoothie

3 passion fruits, inner fruit only

2 cups papaya chunks

2 bananas, frozen

1 cup chopped dandelion greens

1 cup baby spinach leaves

Filtered water and ice

Combine all ingredients in a high speed blender; puree until smooth.

Serves 4

Grapefruit Kiwi Smoothie

2 large grapefruit, peeled and seeds removed

4 kiwifruit, peeled

2 bananas, frozen

1 small cucumber, peeled

1 Tbsp. chia seeds

2 cups fresh chard

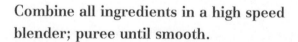

Filtered water and ice

Combine all ingredients in a high speed
blender; puree until smooth.

Serves 4

Sweet Potato Green Smoothie

1 cup raw sweet potato chunks

1 carrot, chopped

1 banana, frozen

1 cup baby spinach leaves

1 cup lettuce leaves (butter or romain)

1/2 tsp. ground cinnamon

1/4 tsp. allspice

1 cup hazelnut or almond milk

Ice

Chopped pecans

Combine all ingredients in a high speed blender; puree until smooth. Garnish individual servings with chopped pecans.

Serves 4

Coconut Piña Colada Smoothie

2 cups fresh chunked pineapple

Meat from 1 young Thai coconut

1 banana, frozen

1/2 – 1 cup coconut milk

Ice

Combine all ingredients in a high speed blender; puree until smooth. Add coconut milk and ice to desired consistency.

Serves 4

Cherry Kiwi Green Smoothie

2 cups fresh cherries, pitted

3 kiwis, skins removed

1 cup chard or beet greens

Juice from 1 lime

1 banana, frozen

1 – 1 ½ cups coconut milk

Combine all ingredients in a high speed blender; puree until smooth. Add coconut milk to desired consistency.

Serves 4

Raw Soups

Raw soups are so easy to make, taste amazing and have healthful benefits galore! The VitaMix blender has a special feature that allows you to heat your soup as you're making it, so you can control the temperature and still have a raw, delicious soup for lunch or dinner.

Mexican Salsa Soup

8 cups chopped fresh tomatoes

3 cups fresh tomato juice

2 medium cucumbers, peeled and chopped

4 large avocados, pitted and skins removed - divided

1 large onion, diced

2 garlic cloves, minced

2 Tbsp. fresh lime juice

2 Tbsp. sliced green onion

1 - 2 jalapeños, seeded and finely diced (to taste)

Sea salt and pepper

Combine chopped tomatoes, tomato juice, cucumbers and 2 of the avocados in a high speed blender; puree until smooth and creamy. Pour mixture into a glass bowl, cover and put in refrigerator. Mash remaining 2 avocados in a large bowl. Add onion, garlic, lime juice, green onion and jalapeños; mix well and season with salt and pepper. Serve chilled soup topped with a spoonful of the avocado mixture.

Serves 6 - 8

Carrot Avocado Ginger Soup

4 cups fresh carrot juice

2 avocados, pits and skins removed

2 Tbsp. minced fresh ginger

2 Tbsp. extra-virgin olive oil

3 Tbsp. Nama Shoyu

1 Tbsp. ground coriander

1/2 cup chopped fresh cilantro

1/4 cup chopped fresh parsley

Sea salt and pepper

1/4 cup sliced green onion

Place carrot juice, avocados and ginger in a high speed blender; blend until well combined. Add olive oil, nama shoyu, coriander, cilantro and parsley; pulse until mixed. Season to taste with salt and pepper.

65

Chill and serve topped with green onions.

Serves 6

Southwestern Corn Chowder

4 cups fresh or frozen corn kernels, divided

3 cups almond milk

1 medium avocado, pitted

1 onion, chopped

2 celery stalks, chopped

1 – 2 chili peppers or jalapeños, seeded and minced (to taste)

2 garlic cloves, minced

2 Tbsp. Nama Shoyu

Sea salt and pepper

1/4 cup chopped fresh cilantro

Combine 2 cups corn, almond milk, avocado, onion, celery, peppers, garlic and nama shoyu in a high speed blender (in batches). Puree until smooth. Add remaining corn

kernels and season with salt and pepper.
Serve topped with cilantro.

Serves 6

Pineapple Gazpacho

6 cups fresh pineapple chunks

4 cups chopped fresh tomatoes

1 medium onion, chopped

1 red bell pepper, seeded and chopped

1 jalapeño, seeded and minced

2 garlic cloves, minced

1/2 cup fresh chopped cilantro

1/4 cup fresh chopped parsley

2 Tbsp. fresh lime juice

2 tsp. chili powder

Sea salt and pepper

Extra virgin olive oil

In a large bowl, combine all ingredients
except for salt and pepper; mix well. In

69

batches, place half the mixture in a high speed blender; blend until smooth and then pour back into the bowl with the chunky mixture. Stir well and season with salt and pepper. Place in refrigerator to chill. Drizzle olive oil on individual servings.

Serves 8

Mango Coconut Ginger Soup

4 cups fresh mango chunks

1 large onion, chopped

1 cup whole coconut milk

2 - 3 chili peppers, seeded and minced (to taste)

2 Tbsp. fresh lime juice

1 Tbsp. minced fresh ginger

Sea salt and pepper

Combine all ingredients except for salt and pepper in a high speed blender (in batches). Puree until smooth and creamy. Add salt and pepper to taste. Chill before serving.

Serves 4 - 6

Creamy Mushroom Soup

4 cups cashew or almond milk

1 onion, chopped

2 garlic cloves, minced

2 cups sliced fresh mushrooms of choice

1 Tbsp. lemon juice

Sea salt and pepper

2 Tbsp. chopped fresh parsley

Extra sliced mushrooms

Combine the cashew or almond milk, onion, garlic, mushrooms and lemon juice in a high speed blender; puree until smooth and season with salt and pepper. Chill soup in refrigerator. Serve topped with fresh parsley and sliced mushrooms.

Serves 4 - 6

Green Vegetable Soup

2 cups baby spinach leaves

1 cup fresh peas, divided

2 medium avocados, pitted

3 cups cashew milk

1 medium onion, diced and divided

Sea salt and pepper

1 Tbsp. fresh chopped parsley

Place spinach leaves, 1/2 cup peas, avocados,
cashew milk and 1/2 the diced onion in a high
speed blender; puree until smooth. Season
with sea salt and pepper. Garnish with
remaining peas, diced onion and parsley.

Serves 4

Mango Salsa Soup

4 cups chopped mangos, divided

1 ½ cups whole coconut milk

Juice from 1 lime

Sea salt and pepper

1 cup diced fresh tomatoes

1 medium avocado, pitted and chopped

1 cucumber, diced

1/4 cup chopped fresh cilantro

Place 3 ½ cups mangos, coconut milk and lime juice in a high speed blender; puree until smooth. Season with sea salt and pepper. Garnish each serving with remaining mango chunks, tomatoes, avocado, cucumber and cilantro.

Serves 4

Orange Pumpkin Spice Soup

3 cups chopped fresh pumpkin

1 ¹/₂ cups fresh orange juice

1 cup almond or cashew milk

5 Medjool dates, soaked for 20 minutes

1 Tbsp. raw honey

1 tsp. ground cinnamon

1/2 tsp. vanilla extract

1/4 tsp. sea salt

Raw pumpkin seeds

Place fresh pumpkin, orange juice, milk, dates, honey, cinnamon, vanilla extract and sea salt in a high speed blender and puree until smooth. Garnish each serving with pumpkin seeds.

Serves 4

Peach Basil Soup

10 medium, ripe peaches, peeled, pitted and chopped

4 cups baby spinach leaves

1/2 cup fresh chopped basil

1 cup almond milk

1/2 cup chopped almonds

Place peaches, spinach leaves, basil and almond milk in a high speed blender; puree until smooth. Garnish each serving with chopped almonds.

Serves 4 – 6

Raw Salads

Raw salads are so amazing, so delicious, and so healthy you may wonder why you haven't been eating them your whole life! The raw dressings give just the right touch of spice and flavor to these recipes.

Apple Lime Ginger Salad

6 cups spring salad greens

2 Fugi or Gala apples, peeled and chopped

1 medium red onion, diced

1/4 cup fresh lime juice

2 Tbsp. fresh ginger, minced

2 Tbsp. chopped fresh cilantro

Sea salt and pepper

Dash of cayenne pepper

Arrange the salad greens on 4 plates. In a bowl, combine the apples, onion, lime juice, ginger and cilantro; stir until well combined. Add salt, pepper and cayenne to taste. Spoon apple mixture on top of salad greens.

Serves 4

Papaya Avocado Salad

5 cups mixed greens

2 medium papayas, pitted and chopped

2 medium avocados, pitted and chopped

Juice from 1 lemon

2 Tbsp. extra virgin olive oil

1 Tbsp. chopped Italian parsley

Sea salt and pepper

Arrange the mixed greens on four serving plates. Sprinkle papayas and avocados over greens. Put lemon juice in a small bowl; whisk in olive oil until emulsified. Stir in parsley. Add sea salt and pepper to taste. Pour over salad.

Serves 4

Summer Coleslaw

1 small head red cabbage

1 small head green cabbage

3 hard pears, shredded

4 carrots, julienned

1/2 cup sliced scallions

2 cups cashews, soaked for at least 2 hours

2 cups cashew milk

Juice and zest from 2 lemons

1 Tbsp. raw honey

Sea salt and pepper

Combine the vegetables and fruit in a large bowl and stir well. Place cashews, cashew milk, lemon juice, zest and honey in a high speed blender; puree until smooth. Add sea salt and pepper to taste; pour over salad and toss to coat.

Serves 6

Jicama Grape Salad with Creamy Cashew Dressing

2 large jicamas, peeled and cubed

2 cups red grapes, each cut in half

1 medium cucumber, cubed

1/4 cup thinly sliced green onion

1 cup Creamy Cashew dressing (below)

In a large bowl combine the jicama, grapes, cucumber, green onion and parsley; mix well.

Creamy Cashew Dressing

1 ½ cups cashews, soaked for 2 hours

Flesh from 2 young coconuts

1/2 – 1/3 cup coconut water

1 Tbsp. chopped fresh parsley

Sea salt and pepper (to taste)

Combine the cashews and coconut flesh in a
high speed blender. Start blending and
slowly add the coconut water through the top
until dressing reaches desired consistency.
Pour into a bowl and stir in parsley and sea
salt to taste. Chill. Serve over Jicama Grape
Salad.

Serves 8

Grapefruit Cranberry Salad with Grapefruit Chia Vinaigrette

5 cups mixed greens

2 large grapefruit, peeled and chopped

1 cup dried cranberries

1 cup chopped almonds

Arrange mixed greens on 4 serving plates. Top with grapefruit pieces, dried cranberries and almonds. Serve with Grapefruit Chia Vinaigrette (below).

Grapefruit Chia Vinaigrette

1/2 cup fresh grapefruit juice

1 Tbsp. raw honey

1 Tbsp. chia seeds

84

1 Tbsp. extra virgin olive oil

Combine all ingredients in a high speed
blender; puree until well mixed. Pour over
Grapefruit Cranberry Salad.

Serves 4

Pear Mixed Greens with Blueberry Vinaigrette

6 cups mixed greens

2 pears, variety of choice, chopped

1 cup cherry tomatoes, halved

1 cup chopped walnuts

Arrange mixed greens on 4 serving plates. Top with chopped pears, cherry tomato halves and chopped walnuts. Top with Blueberry Vinaigrette (below).

Blueberry Vinaigrette

1 cup dried blueberries

1/2 cup extra virgin olive oil

2 Tbsp. raw honey

2 Tbsp. fresh lemon juice

1/4 cup shallots, minced

Sea salt and pepper (to taste)

Combine the dried blueberries, olive oil, honey and lemon juice in a high speed blender; puree until emulsified. Stir in shallots and season with sea salt and pepper. Chill. Pour over Pear Mixed Salad.

Serves 4

Strawberry Pecan Salad with Poppy Seed Vinaigrette

8 cups baby spinach leaves

2 cups sliced fresh strawberries

2 medium cucumbers, thinly sliced

1 cup chopped pecans

Arrange baby spinach on 6 serving plates. Top with strawberries, cucumbers and pecans. Serve with Poppy Seed Vinaigrette (below).

Poppy Seed Vinaigrette

4 Tbsp. raw apple cider vinegar

2 Tbsp. fresh lemon juice

1/2 small red onion, chopped

88

1 tsp. dried mustard

1 Tbsp. raw honey

1/2 cup extra-virgin olive oil

Sea salt and pepper (to taste)

1 $\frac{1}{2}$ Tbsp. poppy seeds

Combine the apple cider vinegar, lemon juice, red onion, dried mustard and honey in a high speed blender; pulse until combined. While blending, slowly drizzle olive oil in through top until emulsified. Season with sea salt and pepper and stir in poppy seeds. Chill. Pour over Strawberry Pecan Salad.

Serves 6

Tomato-Avocado Salad with Creamy Southwest Dressing

4 cups cubed fresh tomatoes

3 medium avocados, pitted and cut in chunks

1 medium cucumber, chopped

1 cup raw corn kernels

1 small red onion, chopped

2 Tbsp. chopped fresh cilantro

Combine all ingredients in a large bowl and stir well. Top with Creamy Southwest Dressing (below).

Creamy Southwest Dressing

1 cup cashews, soaked overnight

1 cup cashew or almond milk

2 garlic cloves

Juice from 2 limes

2 Tbsp. extra virgin olive oil

2 Tbsp. chopped fresh cilantro

1/2 tsp. ground chipotle

Sea salt and pepper (to taste)

Combine all ingredients except for sea salt and pepper in a high speed blender; blend until smooth. Add salt and pepper to taste. Chill. Pour over Tomato-Avocado Salad.

Serves 6

Carrot-Apple Salad with Dill Dressing

4 large carrots, peeled and shredded

3 cups apple chunks

4 stalks celery, finely chopped

1 small onion, diced

In a large bowl, combine all ingredients and mix well. Top with Dill Dressing (below).

Dill Dressing

1 cup cashews, soaked overnight

1/2 cup coconut water

3 Tbsp. raw apple cider vinegar

1 Tbsp. fresh lemon juice

1 Tbsp. extra virgin olive oil

1 tsp. dried mustard

1 Tbsp. fresh dill, finely chopped

Sea salt and pepper (to taste)

Combine all ingredients in a high speed
blender; puree until smooth and creamy.
Chill. Pour over Carrot-Apple Salad.

Serves 6

Tomato Basil Salad

6 cups chopped fresh tomatoes

1 large onion, diced

1 large green bell pepper

1 cup raw cashews, soaked for 2 hours

1 cup cashew milk

1 cup chopped fresh basil

1/2 small onion, chopped

1/4 cup nutritional yeast

1 Tbsp. fresh lime juice

1 $\frac{1}{2}$ tsp. garlic salt

In a large bowl, combine the tomatoes, onion and bell pepper; mix well. In a high speed blender, combine cashews and cashew milk; blend until smooth. Add remaining ingredients and pulse until combined. Pour over tomato mixture.

Serves 4

Marinated Pineapple over Butter Lettuce

1 pineapple, peeled and cut in chunks

2 oranges, juiced (use the zest too)

1/2 tsp. ground cinnamon

1/4 tsp. ground nutmeg

1/8 tsp. ground cloves

1 Tbsp. raw honey

1 head butter lettuce

1 cup walnuts

In a large bowl, combine the pineapple, orange juice and zest, cinnamon, nutmeg, cloves and honey; stir well to coat and set in refrigerator for 2 hours. Arrange butter lettuce on 4 plates. Spoon pineapple and juices over lettuce. Top with walnuts.

Serves 4

Pad Thai with Peanut Sauce

Use a spiral slicer to create the vegetable "noodles" for this dish.

2 medium cucumber (noodles)

2 medium zucchini (noodles)

1 cup red cabbage, thinly sliced

1 large yellow bell pepper, cut in strips

2 carrots, grated

2 cups bean sprouts

1 medium avocado, pitted and sliced

1 cup chopped raw peanuts

1/2 cup sliced scallions

1/2 cup chopped fresh cilantro

Arrange vegetables onto 4 serving plates and

sprinkle with peanuts, scallions and cilantro. Serve with Peanut Sauce (below).

Peanut Sauce

1 cup raw peanut butter

2 garlic cloves

1 inch piece of fresh ginger

Juice from 2 lemons

3 Tbsp. raw honey

2 Tbsp. Nama Shoyu

1/4 cup extra virgin olive oil

Water

Cayenne pepper

Place all ingredients except for water and cayenne pepper in a high speed blender.

Start blending and slowly add the water through the top until sauce reaches desired consistency (you'll use about 1/2 – 1/3 cup). Add the cayenne pepper to taste. Drizzle sauce over each salad.

Serves 4

Basil-Mint Fruit Salad

2 cups fresh sliced strawberries

2 cups fresh blueberries

2 cups fresh chopped mango

2 cups cubed cantaloupe

2 cups chopped pears

1 cup chopped kiwifruit

1/4 cup chopped fresh basil

Juice from 2 large lemons

1 Tbsp. raw honey

1/4 cup chopped fresh mint

Combine fruit in a large bowl. Sprinkle basil
over fruit and stir. Combine lemon juice,
honey and mint; pour over fruit, stir.

Serves 8 - 10

101

Grapefruit-Papaya Kale Salad

5 cups chopped kale greens

1 large grapefruit, peeled and chopped

1 papaya, peeled, seeded and chopped

1 medium cucumber, chopped

1 small red onion, thinly sliced

1 cup cashews, soaked for at least 2 hours

1/2 cup water

Juice from 2 limes

1 inch piece fresh ginger

1/4 cup chopped fresh cilantro

Arrange kale on 4 serving plates. Top with
grapefruit, papaya, cucumber and red onion.
Place the cashews, water, lime juice, ginger
and cilantro in a high speed blender; puree
until smooth. Pour over salad.

Serves 4

Cucumber-Tomato Salsa Salad

3 medium cucumbers, diced

3 cups chopped fresh tomatoes

2 stalks celery, diced

1 green bell pepper, seeded and diced

1 small onion, diced

1/4 cup chopped fresh Italian parsley

Juice from 1 lemon

Extra virgin olive oil

Sea salt and pepper

In a large bowl place cucumbers, tomatoes, celery, bell pepper, onion and parsley; mix well. Drizzle lemon juice and olive oil over vegetables. Season with sea salt and pepper.

Serves 4

Watermelon Arugula Salad

5 cups arugula greens

2 cups chopped watermelon

2 medium cucumbers

Fresh chopped parsley

Juice from 1 lemon

3 Tbsp. extra virgin olive oil

Sea salt and pepper

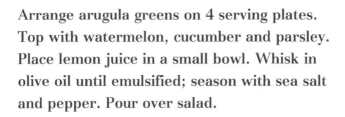

Arrange arugula greens on 4 serving plates.
Top with watermelon, cucumber and parsley.
Place lemon juice in a small bowl. Whisk in
olive oil until emulsified; season with sea salt
and pepper. Pour over salad.

Serves 4

Raw Main Dishes

Raw main dishes are affordable, easy to prepare and a great way to boost your health. Feel free to experiment with different combinations of vegetables and fruits.

Zucchini Noodles with Spinach-Cashew Sauce

Use a spiral slicer to create the zucchini "noodles" for this dish.

2 medium zucchini (noodles)

2 cups asparagus, cut into 1 inch pieces

1 cup fresh sliced mushrooms

1 cup cherry tomatoes, halved

1 small red onion, thinly sliced

1 red bell pepper, thinly sliced

1/2 cup dried cranberries

2 cups baby spinach leaves

1 cup cashews, soaked overnight

1 garlic clove

1 Tbsp. fresh lemon juice

1/4 cup extra virgin olive oil

1/4 – 1/2 cup water

Sea salt and pepper

In a large bowl, combine zucchini noodles, asparagus, mushrooms, tomatoes, red onion, bell pepper and dried cranberries; toss well. Combine spinach, cashews, garlic, lemon juice and olive oil in a high speed blender. Turn on and slowly pour in water through the top until sauce reaches desired consistency. Season with sea salt and pepper and pour over zucchini-vegetable mixture. Toss to coat.

Serves 4

"Completely" Raw Sushi

Yes, you can create raw sushi! For the rice, you can use bean sprouts, sprouted kamut or raw parsnips (pulsed in a food processor), or you can simply create rolls with strips of vegetables without the imitation rice. There are countless ways and ingredients you can use – try experimenting with different combinations!

"Rice" of choice

1 medium avocado, pitted and cut in thin strips

1 red or yellow bell pepper, cut in thin strips

2 medium cucumbers, cut in thin strips

Mushrooms of choice, thinly sliced

Green onions, thinly sliced

Herbs – cilantro, parsley, basil

109

4 Nori (seaweed) sheets

Sauces for Dipping:

Nama Shoyu

Fresh Ginger Sauce: blend fresh ginger with water in a high speed food processor.

Tahini Sauce:

1/4 cup raw tahini

1/4 cup extra virgin olive oil

1/4 cup chopped fresh cilantro

2 Tbsp. fresh lemon juice

2 Tbsp. coconut milk

2 garlic cloves

1 tsp. raw honey

Sea salt and pepper

For the Sushi:

Place a roll of Nori on a cutting board. Place any combination of "rice" and vegetables across the bottom of the sheet. Using dampened fingers, gently roll into a sushi roll. Using a sharp knife, cut into pieces and arrange on a plate. Top with sauce of choice.

For the Tahini Sauce:

Combine all ingredients in a high speed blender; puree until smooth seasoning with sea salt and pepper.

Serves 4 – 6

Raw Herbed Veggie Burgers

1 cup walnuts, soaked for 2 hours

1 cup sunflower seeds, soaked for 2 hours

1 small onion, chopped

1 garlic clove

1/2 red bell pepper, chopped

1 Tbsp. fresh oregano

1 Tbsp. fresh parsley

Water

Sea salt and pepper

Combine walnuts, sunflower seeds, onion, garlic, bell pepper, oregano and parsley in a food processor. Slowly add water and pulse until mixture comes together but is not overly sticky. Season with sea salt and pepper. Shape into 4 patties and place in dehydrator at 115° for 3 hours. Serve on lettuce leaves

112

or between dehydrated "buns" (next recipe).

Serves 4

Raw "Buns" for Veggie Burgers and Sandwiches

2 cups almonds, pulsed to a fine meal

1 cup almond flour

4 prunes, soaked for 20 minutes

2 Tbsp. flax meal

2 Tbsp. sunflower seeds

2 Tbsp. extra virgin olive oil

1 tsp. dried herb mixture (such as oregano, thyme, sage, marjoram, etc.)

Sea salt and pepper

Water

Sesame seeds

Combine all ingredients except for water and sesame seeds in a food processor; pulse until well combined. Add water a little at a time until mixture comes together, but isn't sticky. Shape into balls and flatten with your hand to create a bun shape. Sprinkle sesame seeds on top and gently press into buns. Place on a dehydrator sheet and dehydrate at 105° for about 7 hours or until buns are dry but not crumbly. Store in refrigerator until ready to use.

Serves 4

Pesto over Yellow Squash

Use a spiral slicer to create the yellow squash "noodles" for this dish.

3 medium yellow squash (noodles)

2 cups fresh basil leaves

1 cup pine nuts, walnuts, cashews or almonds

4 garlic cloves, minced

2 tsp. fresh lemon juice

1/3 cup extra virgin olive oil

1/4 cup nutritional yeast

Sea salt and pepper

Arrange yellow squash "noodles" on 4 serving plates. Combine basil, nuts, garlic, lemon juice, yeast, and olive oil in a food processor; pulse until mixture is combined.

Season with sea salt and pepper. Spoon pesto mixture over yellow squash.

Serves 4

Curried Cabbage with Brazil Nuts and Apples

1 large head green cabbage, thinly sliced

3 Tbsp. Nama Shoyu

3 Tbsp. extra virgin olive oil

Juice from 2 lemons

1 tsp. curry powder

1/2 tsp. ground cumin

1/2 cup chopped Brazil nuts

1 large apple, peeled and chopped

In a large bowl, combine the cabbage, Nama Shoyu, olive oil, lemon juice, curry powder and cumin; stir until well combined. Arrange cabbage mixture on 4 serving plates. Top with Brazil nuts and apple chunks.

Serves 4

Italian Spaghetti

Use a spiral slicer to create the zucchini "noodles" for this dish.

2 medium zucchini (noodles)

4 cups diced fresh tomatoes

1 small onion, chopped

1 green bell pepper, chopped

2 garlic cloves

1 Tbsp. raw honey or agave nectar

Juice from 2 lemons

1/2 cup extra virgin olive oil

1/2 cup chopped fresh basil

2 Tbsp. chopped fresh oregano

Sea salt and pepper

Extra chopped basil

Arrange zucchini "noodles" on 4 serving plates. Combine the tomatoes, onion, bell pepper, garlic, honey or agave, lemon juice, olive oil, basil and oregano in a food processor; blend until smooth. Season with sea salt and pepper. Pour sauce over zucchini and garnish with chopped basil.

Serves 4

Mexican Lettuce Wraps

3 cups diced fresh tomatoes

2 medium avocados, pitted and chopped

1 small onion, diced

1 yellow or red bell pepper, chopped

1 medium cucumber, diced

2 garlic cloves, minced

1 Serrano pepper, seeded and minced

 1/4 cup fresh chopped cilantro

Juice from 2 limes

1 tsp. agave nectar

Sea salt and pepper

Romaine or iceberg lettuce leaves

In a large bowl combine tomatoes, avocados, onion, bell pepper, cucumber, garlic,

Serrano pepper, cilantro, lime juice and agave; stir well. Season with sea salt and pepper. Scoop a spoonful of tomato mixture onto a lettuce leaf. Wrap and serve.

Serves 4 – 6

Fennel Hash with Hazelnuts and Figs

Use a mandoline slicer to create thin fennel shavings for this dish.

2 medium fennel bulbs, green tops and bulbs removed, sliced in half down the middle, thinly shaved

2 pears, pitted and diced

2 carrots, julienned

1 shallot, minced

Juice from 1 lemon

2 Tbsp. olive oil

Sea salt and pepper

1/2 cup hazelnuts, coarsely chopped

8 fresh figs, quartered

In a large bowl, combine fennel, pears, carrots and shallots; mix well. Drizzle lemon juice and olive oil over all, and season with sea salt and pepper; toss to coat. Arrange fennel mixture on 4 serving plates. Top with hazelnuts and figs.

Serves 4

Asian Carrot Noodles

Use a spiral slicer to create the carrot "noodles" for this dish.

4 medium carrots (noodles)

1/2 cup thinly sliced mushrooms

1/4 cup green onions, sliced

Juice from 2 lemons

1 garlic clove

1 inch piece of fresh ginger

1 Tbsp. tahini

1 Tbsp. extra virgin olive oil

2 tsp. Nama Shoyu

Chopped fresh parsley

Sesame seeds

In a large bowl combine the carrots, mushrooms and green onion; mix well. Arrange on 4 serving plates. Combine the lemon juice, garlic, ginger, tahini, olive oil and Nama Shoyu in a high speed blender; puree until smooth. Pour over carrot mixture. Garnish with fresh parsley and sesame seeds.

Serves 4

Mushroom Meatballs over Heirloom Tomatoes

2 cups mushrooms of choice, coarsely chopped

1 $1/2$ cups walnuts

1 medium carrot, chopped

1 small onion, chopped

1 garlic clove

2 Tbsp. flax meal

1 Tbsp. extra virgin olive oil

1 Tbsp. chopped fresh parsley

2 tsp. chopped fresh thyme

1 tsp. chopped fresh oregano

1/4 tsp. sea salt

1/8 tsp. black pepper

Water

3 large heirloom tomatoes, diced

Sea salt and pepper

Place the mushrooms, walnuts, carrot, onion, garlic, flax meal, olive oil, parsley, thyme, oregano, sea salt and pepper in a food processor; pulse until mixture comes together but is not sticky. You may need to add some water to create the desired consistency. Shape into 1 inch "meatballs" and place on a dehydrator sheet. Dehydrate at 110° for about 7 hours. Arrange heirloom tomatoes on 4 serving plates and season with sea salt and pepper. Place meatballs on top of tomatoes.

Serves 4

Sweet Potato & Cucumber with Avocado Sauce

2 large sweet potatoes, shredded

2 medium cucumbers, shredded

2 medium avocados, pitted

1 large tomato

1 garlic clove

Juice of 1 lime

Dash of cayenne pepper

Sea salt and pepper

Arrange the sweet potatoes and cucumbers on 4 serving plates. Combine the avocados, tomato, garlic, lime juice and cayenne pepper in a food processor; pulse until mixture comes together. Season with sea salt and pepper. Pour over vegetables.

Serves 4

129

Veggie Collard Green Wraps

2 tomatoes, chopped

2 medium cucumbers, chopped

5 radishes, thinly sliced

3 carrots, grated

1/2 cup sliced green onion

Juice from 1 lemon

1 Tbsp. extra virgin olive oil

Sea salt and pepper

Collard green leaves

In a large bowl, combine the tomatoes,
cucumbers, radishes, carrots, green onion,
lemon juice and olive oil; toss to coat. Season
with sea salt and pepper. Spoon some of the
veggie mixture into a collard green leaf.
Wrap and serve.

Serves 4

Portabella Tacos with Salsa

Meat:

8 large portabella mushrooms, diced

4 Tbsp. ground cashews

4 Tbsp. sundried tomatoes, minced

3 garlic cloves, minced

2 tsp. chili powder

2 tsp. cumin

Sea salt (to taste)

Salsa:

4 cups chopped roma tomatoes

1 large onion, diced

1 large green bell pepper, diced

2 jalapeños, ribs and seeds removed, diced

1 cup chopped fresh cilantro

2 avocados, pitted and cut in small chunks

Sea salt (to taste)

Lettuce leaves (romaine or iceberg)

For the meat: In a large bowl combine the portabellas, cashews, sundried tomatoes, garlic, chili powder and cumin; mix well. Add sea salt to taste. Set aside.

For the salsa: In a large bowl combine all ingredients and stir well. Add sea salt to taste.

Spoon some of the meat into a lettuce leaf. Top with salsa and serve.

Serves 6 – 8

Raw Desserts

Raw desserts are so delicious, so nutritious; you won't feel bad about having a second helping.

Chocolate Almond-Hazelnut Pudding

4 medium avocados

1 cup hazelnut butter

2 cups almond milk

1 ¼ cups cacao powder

1 cup agave nectar

1 tsp. almond extract

Chopped almonds

Combine all ingredients in a food processor; blend until very smooth and creamy. Refrigerate several hours before serving. Sprinkle chopped almonds on individual servings.

Serves 8

Lemon Strawberry Cheesecake

Crust:

1 ¹/₂ cups almonds

1/2 cup almond flour

5 Medjool dates, soaked for 3 hours

1 - 2 Tbsp. extra virgin coconut oil

Filling:

2 ¹/₂ cups cashews, soaked 3 hours or overnight

1/2 cup fresh lemon juice (about 3 lemons)

2 Tbsp. lemon zest (from lemons)

2/3 cup agave nectar

3/4 cup coconut butter

2 cups chopped fresh strawberries

For the crust: Combine the almonds, almond flour and dates in a food processor. Pulse and slowly add the coconut oil until mixture sticks together and is right consistency for a crust. Press into a 9 inch spring form pan.

For the filling: Combine all ingredients except for strawberries in a food processor; process until mixture is smooth and creamy. Fold in strawberries and pour over crust. Refrigerate 3 – 4 hours before serving.

Serves 8 - 10

Festive Walnut Fudge

1 1/2 cups almond butter

1 cup hazelnut butter

1 cup cacao powder

1/3 cup agave nectar

4 Tbsp. extra virgin coconut oil, plus more for greasing the baking dish

1/2 tsp. vanilla extract

1 cup chopped walnuts

In a large bowl combine almond butter, cacao, agave, coconut oil and vanilla; mix well. Stir in walnuts. Lightly grease a 9x13 baking dish with coconut oil. Press mixture into the dish. Place in the refrigerator for several hours.

Makes about 70 small pieces

Maple Oat Apple Cinnamon Cookies

4 cups raw flaked oats

2 cups applesauce

2 cups oat flour

1 cup extra virgin coconut oil

1/2 cup pure maple syrup

2 tsp. ground cinnamon

In a large bowl combine first three ingredients; mix well. Add remaining ingredients and stir until well combined. Drop by rounded tablespoon onto a dehydrator sheet. Using the bottom of a glass, slightly flatten each cookie. Place in dehydrator at 145° for 40 minutes, and then reduce the temperature to 115° and continue dehydrating for about 6 hours or until cookies are soft and chewy.

Makes about 3 dozen cookies

Grasshopper Pie

Crust:

1 cup hazelnuts

1/4 cup cacao powder

3 dates, soaked for 3 or more hours

1 Tbsp. extra virgin coconut oil

Filling:

3 medium avocados

1 cup cashews, soaked overnight

1 cup baby spinach leaves

1 cup young coconut flesh

1/4 cup extra virgin coconut oil

1/2 cup agave nectar

Food grade peppermint essential oil

Ganache:

1/4 cup cacao powder

1/4 cup raw honey

1 – 2 Tbsp. extra virgin coconut oil

For the crust: Combine ingredients in a food processor and pulse until mixture comes together. Press into a 9 inch pie plate.

For the filling: Combine ingredients in a food processor and blend until smooth. Add a few drops of peppermint essential oil to taste. Pour into crust. Refrigerate 2 – 3 hours.

For the Ganache: In a small bowl, combine the ingredients and whisk until smooth, using enough coconut oil for the right consistency. Drizzle over chilled pie.

Serves 8

Coconut Banana Cream Pie

Crust:

1 ¹/₂ cups pecans

1 cup walnuts

5 Medjool dates, soaked overnight

2 Tbsp. coconut butter

Filling:

2 cups cashews, soaked 5 hours or overnight

1 cup coconut flesh (from young coconut)

1 cup shredded coconut, divided

1/4 cup whole coconut milk

1/4 cup coconut butter

1/4 cup raw honey

1/2 tsp. vanilla extract

2 ripe bananas

142

For the crust: Blend pecans and walnuts in a food processor until crumbly. Add dates and coconut butter; pulse until combined. Press into a 9 inch pie plate.

For the Filling: Combine cashews, coconut flesh, 1/2 cup shredded coconut, coconut milk and coconut butter in a food processor; blend well. Blend in honey and vanilla. Add bananas one at a time, blending until mixture is light and fluffy. Pour into pie crust and sprinkle remaining 1/2 cup shredded coconut on top. Refrigerate for several hours before serving.

Serves 8

Basic Chocolate Truffles with Variations

2 cups almond butter

1 cup cacao powder

1/2 cup raw honey or agave nectar

Place all ingredients in a food processor; blend until well combined. Add a variation.

Variations:

Dried Fruit (apricots, cranberries, cherries)

Cacao powder

Shredded coconut

Finely chopped nuts of choice

Place a piece of dried fruit in the center of truffle and roll chocolate around it. Or, roll truffles into balls and roll in cacao powder, shredded coconut or nuts.

Makes about 2 dozen truffles

Coconut Chia Pudding with Blackberries

3 ½ cups coconut milk

1 cup chia seeds

3/4 cup raw honey

1 tsp. pure vanilla extract

1 tsp. ground cinnamon

1 ½ cups blackberries, washed and dried

Combine coconut milk, chia seeds, honey, vanilla and cinnamon; stir well and set aside for about 15 minutes to thicken. Fold in blackberries. Refrigerate.

Serves 8

Raspberry Mint Ice Cream

Mint Cream:

4 cups cashews, soaked overnight and drained

4 cups coconut water (or water)

2/3 cup fresh chopped mint

Ice Cream:

4 cups mint cream

1 cup almond milk

1 cup agave nectar

2 cups fresh raspberries

For the mint cream: Place cashews and coconut water in a blender; blend until smooth. Add mint and puree until smooth. Pour mixture into a dish and refrigerate.

For the ice cream: Combine mint cream, almond milk and agave. Pour mixture into an ice cream maker and turn on; let churn until thick. Slightly crush raspberries using a potato masher; stir into ice cream. Place in a container and freeze until ready to serve.

Serves 8

Hazelnut Cinnamon Cacao Brownies

2 cups hazelnuts

1 cup cacao powder

1 tsp. pure vanilla extract

1 tsp. ground cinnamon

1/8 tsp. sea salt

2 cups Medjool dates

1/2 cup dried figs

Ganache:

1/2 cup cacao powder

1/2 cup raw honey

1/4 cup extra virgin coconut oil

1/2 tsp. cinnamon

149

Place hazelnuts in a food processor; pulse until finely chopped. Add vanilla, cinnamon and sea salt; mix. Slowly add the dates and figs until mixture is combined and has a consistent texture. Press into an 8x8 baking dish. For the ganache, combine all ingredients and mix well. Pour over brownies. Refrigerate until set.

Makes about sixteen 2 inch brownies

Carrot Zucchini Apple Pie

Crust:

3 medium carrots, peeled and grated

1/2 cup pecans

1/2 cup almonds

1/2 cup dates, soaked for 2 hours

1/2 cup golden raisins

1/2 tsp. ground cinnamon

1/2 tsp. ground ginger

1/2 tsp. ground nutmeg

Filling:

5 tart apples, such as Granny Smith

2 cups finely grated zucchini

3 Tbsp. agave nectar

2 Tbsp. flax meal

1 tsp. fresh lemon juice

1 tsp. ground cinnamon

For the crust: Combine crust ingredients in a food processor; pulse until crumbly. Press into a 9 inch pie plate and put in refrigerator.

For the filling: Peel and core apples; place in a food processor. Add zucchini, agave, flax meal, lemon juice and cinnamon; pulse until ingredients are well combined. Pour mixture into pie crust and refrigerate for several hours.

Serves 8

Decadent Chocolate Mousse with Raspberries

1 ¹/₂ cups dates, pits removed

4 medium avocados

2 cups coconut milk

1/2 cup raw peanut butter

1/2 cup raw almond butter

1 1/4 cup cacao powder

1/2 cup agave nectar

Fresh raspberries

Soak dates for several hours or until very soft. Combine all ingredients in a food processor or blender; puree until smooth and creamy. Chill in refrigerator. Serve topped with fresh raspberries.

Serves 8

Nutty Apple Apricot Crisp

1 cup pecans

1 cup walnuts

1 cup almonds

4 cups raw flaked oats

2 cups fresh apples, peeled and chopped

2 cups fresh apricots, pitted and chopped

1/4 cup extra virgin coconut oil

1 cup raw honey

Combine pecans, walnuts and almonds in a
food processor; pulse until coarsely chopped
and transfer to a large bowl. Add remaining
ingredients and mix well. Pour mixture into 8
individual 1 cup ramekins. Dehydrate at 145°
for about 40 minutes and then reduce
temperature to 115°. Continue dehydrating

for 3 – 4 more hours.

Serves 8

Almond Cranberry Macaroons

1/4 cup almonds

1/4 cup almond flour

2 cups shredded unsweetened coconut

1/2 cup dried cranberries

1/2 cup agave nectar

1/4 cup extra virgin coconut oil

1/2 tsp. vanilla extract

Place almonds in a food processor; pulse until crumbly. Add almond flour, shredded coconut, cranberries, agave, coconut oil and vanilla; pulse until mixture clumps together. Shape into 2 inch balls and place on a sheet in dehydrator. Dehydrate at 115° for about 6 – 7 hours, or until the consistency of cookies are soft and chewy.

Makes about 2 dozen cookies

Thank you for enjoying this cookbook!

ABOUT THE AUTHOR

Abby Richards loves cooking raw for her family. Even her kids love the food and she is happy knowing she is providing good, healthy meals for them. She lives with her family and cat in Arizona.

Printed in Great Britain
by Amazon.co.uk, Ltd.,
Marston Gate.